GOLF ON GULLANE HILL

A celebration of 100 years of Gullane Golf Club

ARCHIE BAIRD

COPY NO.

2nd Edition 1985
3rd Edition 1989 (enlarged)
4th Edition 1992 (enlarged)

ISBN 0 9515200 0 8

This edition sponsored by
Douglas M. Kinney and
Palmer Capital Corporation, Chicago, Illinois

Printed by Macdonald Lindsay Pindar plc
Edgefield Road
Loanhead
Midlothian EH20 9SY

Contents

	Page
Chapter 1 *The making of the links*	7
Wind, Sand and Rock	7
Rabbits	7
Wool	8
Feathers	8
Saved by Gum!	9
Chapter 2 *The Fall and Rise of Gullane*	10
Choked by Sand	10
Horses or Courses?	11
Chapter 3 *The East Lothian Golf Club*	12
Farmers and Brewers	12
Medal and Match	13
Sheep's Head and Haggis	13
Morning Toddy	15
Wind and Snow	15
Genial and Noble	17
Chapter 4 *Dirleton Castle Golf Club*	18
Secretary and Landlord	18
Smiddy and Pond	18
Toast and Song	19
County Cup	19
Actual and Nominal	21
A Ripple on the Pool	22
Two Wins and a Loss	23
Two Stalwarts	24
Chapter 5 *Gullane Golf Club*	25
Grass Very Rank	25
Manly and Intellectual	25
Differences	26
Adjusted!	27
A New Course	27
No. 3 for £1,000!	28
Inflation	28
New Clubhouse	28
Half Wages	29
Sheep and no Water	29

Two Green Staff 29
Six Strike 30
Lloyd George 30
Sunday Golf. 30
Women Weeders 30
Light Relief 30
Derby Cup 30
Offer to Sell Courses 30
New Clubhouse 31
Purchase of Courses 32
The Thirties 32
Gifts and Scores 33
Sell the Horse 34
Bullets, Bombs and Blocks 35
Water Colours and Whisky 35
Silver and Balls 36
The Fifties 36
Fortunes Improve. 37
The Match Dinners 38

Chapter 6 *Tournaments and Champions* 40

Chapter 7 *Other Clubs* 42
The Gullane Golfers 42
The Hanky-Panky Golfers 42
The Roundel Club 43
The Harum-Scarum Club 43
The Gullane Nine Club 43
Gullane Comrades 45

Chapter 8 *Greenkeepers* 48

Chapter 9 *The Ladies* 52
Dancing and Tea 52
British Ladies 1897 52
British Ladies 1947 53
Roll of Honour 57

Chapter 10 *Various Praise* 59
Club Champions 65
Captains 66

Postscript 68

Gullane Links by J. Smart, R.S.A. 1888.

List of Illustrations

Winter Sports (Kilted Figures playing golf) by Adriaen van de Velde. . . . 8
The Evolution of the Golf Ball. . . . 9
Map I. . . . 10
Semi-Finals Day.. . . . 11
"The Lonely Golfer" by John R. Barclay. . . . 12
"A Fine Shot!" by John R. Barclay. . . . 14
Gullane Old Clubhouse. . . . 16
"Two Golfers" by John R. Barclay. . . . 17
Map II. . . . 20
Map III. . . . 22
T. D. Thomson, Captain 1884-1886. . . . 26
Willie Park Junior. . . . 27
Map IV. . . . 29
A. W. Robertson Durham, Lord Derby and Major Smith (Secy.). . . 31
East Links, Gullane—"Hens in the Bunker." . . . 33
James Dishington, Greenkeeper. . . . 34
Alex Aitken's Shop. . . . 37
Reflections. . . . 39
R. Reid Jack. . . . 41
Menu Card, Gullane Nine Club. J. D. H. McIntosh, Captain. . . 44
Hugh Watt, Gullane Comrades, winner with Tom Dobson of the "Evening Times" Trophy, 1923. . . . 46
W. R. Clapperton, Captain, 1882-1884.. . . . 49
"A Difficult Lie?" by John R. Barclay. . . . 51
"Babe" Zaharias, British Ladies Champion, 1947. . . . 53
British Ladies' Championship at Gullane, by Michael Brown.. . . 54
Key to the picture by Michael Brown. . . . 55
Jean Anderson (Donald). . . . 57
"Well Away" by John R. Barclay.. . . . 64
Earliest Competition of the Club.. . . . 67

ACKNOWLEDGEMENTS

My gratitude must be expressed for a wide variety of help and encouragement.

The Captain, Committee and Secretary of Gullane Golf Club, Gullane Ladies Golf Club, The East Lothian Golf Club, Dirleton Castle Golf Club, The Gullane Nine Golf Club and Gullane Comrades for access to their Minute Books.

The Captain, Council and Secretary of Luffness New Golf Club for permission to reproduce the painting by John Smart.

My thanks also go to Stewart Kinnear, Jim Still, Stanley Eveling and Ian Grant for special knowledge and advice. To Alistair Adamson, George Colville and Ian Henderson for editing and example.

To Jack Park, "Shaig" Logan, Jean Anderson, Barbara McIntosh, Reid Jack, Dick Smith and Sandy Williamson for their memories.

To Irene Sutherland for transforming my garbled tapes into neat typing, and to Una Kerr for research.

To Jack Crombie for many fine photographs.

To Ian McNee and Macdonalds for their excellent printing.

Financial help has come from—and I thank

The Bank of Scotland,

Scottish & Newcastle Breweries Ltd., and

Ransomes Grass Machinery (Scotland) Ltd.

Finally, to my dear wife Sheila who has been a source of inspiration and a pillar of patience, as well as producing the colour slides.

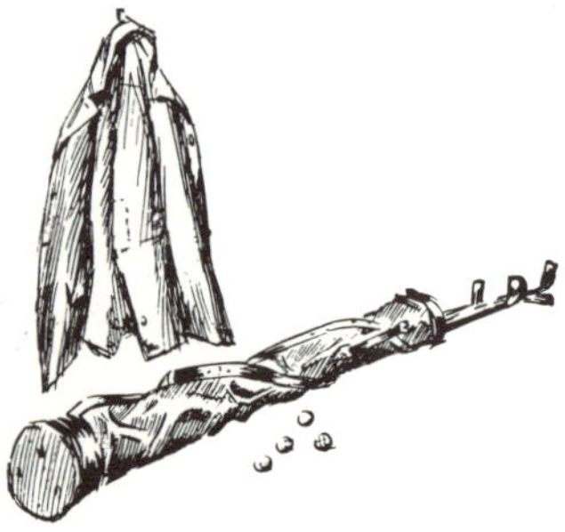

1

THE MAKING OF THE LINKS

Golf has been played on Gullane links for over 300 years. As far back as 1650, the weavers of Dirleton played the weavers of Aberlady annually on Old Handsel Monday. However, there was no organised club until early last century, when some local farmers banded together to play golf. This club became defunct about the end of the feather ball period (1848) but it was resuscitated in 1859 and, as the East Lothian Golf Club, still holds meetings today at Gullane.

The oldest club in continuous existence at Gullane is Dirleton Castle, founded in 1854 by "shopkeepers, working men and artisans".

Weavers; farmers; artisans; their appreciation of Nature's golfing bounty at Gullane has spread world-wide.

Golf on Gullane Hill was a lucky combination of wind, sand, rock, rabbits, wool, feathers and gum.

Wind, Sand and Rock

As the tide ebbed and Aberlady Bay emptied, the prevailing west wind dried off the sand and each day blew millions of grains against the plug of basalt rock which forms the core of Gullane Hill. Over the centuries, the gently undulating contours were stabilised by marram and bent grass followed by lichens and mosses and, as the salt was washed through the sand, fescues became established.

Rabbits

The wind and sand set the stage; now enter the heroes: rabbits. They found the fescues to their taste, the sand easy to burrow and few rivals for the vast area. They congregated in the shallow depressions where the dew and the rain collected and the grass was a little sweeter, and they cropped it to a lawn-like smoothness. If they found a succulent new shoot of hawthorn or buckthorn had taken root, they applied their sharp little incisors and "nipped it in the bud."

They kept the links-land free from bushes and shrubs although the seeds were continually trying to make a start. The importance of rabbits was clearly shown when the myxomatosis virus almost wiped them out in 1956 and hawthorn and buckthorn sprang up all over the hill. Although the virus re-appeared regularly, it has never repeated the earlier decimation and the status quo seems to have been restored.

This terrain at Gullane became known as links or links-land. These links-lands were common on the east coast of Scotland, from Dunbar to Dornoch.

Wool

Before 1800 Scotland's main export was wool. The best market was Holland and in Holland the Dutch have records of a game like golf from 1300. Scotland's earliest golfing records do not go back before 1450. Scottish sailors and merchants, as well as the many mercenary soldiers, spent much time in Holland and became involved in Dutch life. See "Kilted Figures playing golf." Adriaen van de Velde (1668).

Winter Sports (Kilted Figures playing golf) by Adriaen van de Velde, 1668.

The game spread from the frozen canals, the fields, and the streets of Holland to the links near the harbours of Dunbar, North Berwick, Aberlady, Musselburgh, Leith, Leven, St Andrews, Carnoustie, Montrose, Aberdeen and Dornoch. These were the early golf courses and from 1450 to 1850 the game existed almost exclusively on the east coast of Scotland.

Feathers

The only ball available was the "feathery"—a stitched leather case, stuffed with a top-hat full of feathers. It took a skilled man half a day to make one. The ball, which cost more than a club, was easily damaged and its cost controlled the popularity of the game.

Saved by Gum

Not until 1850 did a viable alternative appear. This was a tropical gum called gutta-percha. It could be moulded when warm but became hard and resilient when cool. It was cheap and durable, and golf expanded quickly—everyone could now afford to play.

Very Old Feather Ball

Old Gourlay Feather Ball

Old Gutta Ball (smooth)

Early Park Gutta Ball (slightly nicked)

Early Dunn Gutta Ball (hand-hammered)

Hand-hammered Gutta

Gourlay Gutta Ball (hand-hammered)

A Modern Gutta Ball

THE EVOLUTION OF THE GOLF-BALL

2

THE FALL AND RISE OF GULLANE

Choked by Sand

The sand which blew off Aberlady Bay had, in the 16th and 17th centuries, nearly choked the village of Gullane. St Andrew's Church, the ruins of which are just behind the first tee of Gullane No. 1 course, had been founded about 1150, made collegiate (endowed with sufficient funds to support two priests) about 1450 but was demoted in 1750 because of the diminishing size and importance of the village.

However, once golf began to grow the village prospered. From the original three or four holes near the old church, the course was stretched

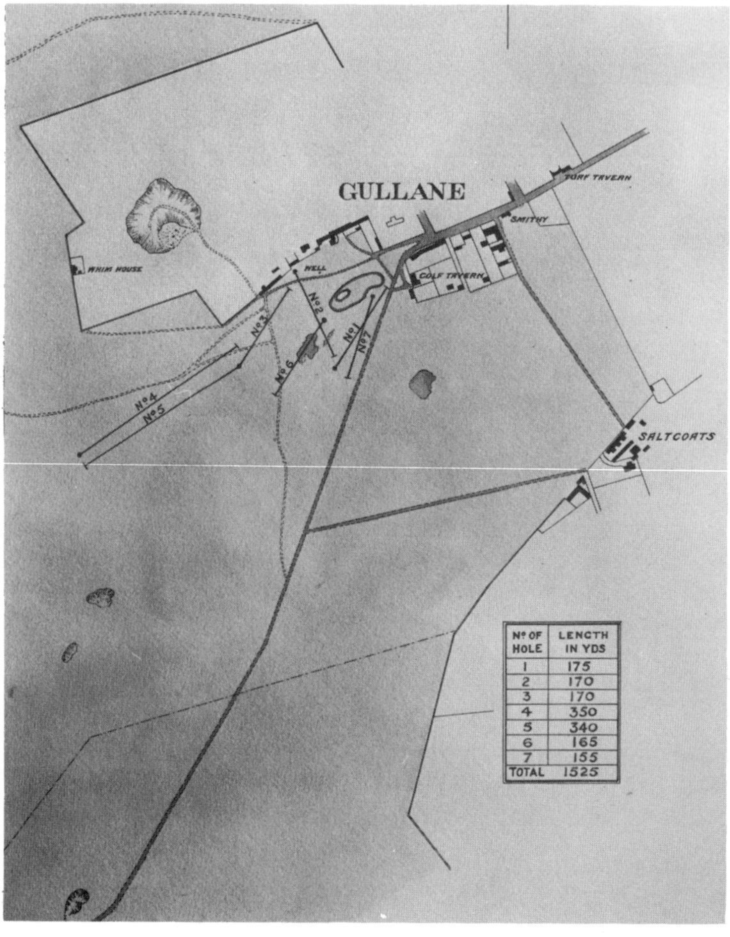

Map I shows the original seven holes, c. 1840. They start and finish beside "The Pond."

steadily until by 1910 there were three fine 18-hole courses and, in addition, a children's course where the old four holes used to be.

Horses or Courses

This progress was not made without opposition. There had been, over 50 years – from 1842 to 1892 – a serious threat to golf on the hill. Gullane was an important and successful training area for race horses and exercising them on the hill was a well-established practice. But in a lengthy judgment in 1892, Lord Low prohibited exercising and training on Gullane Hill and by this judgment made the hill permanently available for golf.

Guy Robertson Durham, "Squiggles" Mackie, Charles Lawrie and Jack Ness, 5th Green.

3

EAST LOTHIAN GOLF CLUB

Farmers and Brewers

Farmers of the district and their Edinburgh friends made up the club. A study of the Minutes suggests that the farmers raised barley for the Edinburgh members, who were mostly brewers, with the names of Aitchison, Dryburgh, Usher and McEwan prominent.

It was a very sociable club. Lunch and dinner were an important part of their meetings and many of the Minutes were given to describing the fare and the fun.

They played only on Gullane Hill for the first 16 years of their revival. Indeed one of the rules in their first Minutes was "the place for playing to be on Gullane Hill." In 1875 they started to play the Spring Meeting at Archerfield, the estate at the other end of the village and, in 1883 they

"The Lonely Golfer" by John R. Barclay.

played at North Berwick. In 1897 they held their Summer Meeting at New Luffness "because Gullane was so crowded on a Saturday." (This may be a suitable place to insert a quotation from The Golfing Annual of 1890.) "Luffness putting greens are excellent, though it must be admitted in justice to its neighbour and rival Gullane, they are hardly up to the unequalled greens on the links there, where the turf is as smooth as velvet and perfect in every respect."

This, of course, refers to Old Luffness, the course which used to lie just over the timber bridge, in front of Luffness House. (The story of Old Luffness, Kilspindie and New Luffness must wait for another book.)

Medal and Match

They also met and played at the invitation of St Clair Cunningham (he was secretary) at his private course at Hedderwick Hill near Dunbar in June, 1897, again in 1899 and 1902 when "the green was found to be in grand order." But the great majority of their gatherings were at the Golf Hotel in Gullane and their play on Gullane Hill. Their day began with a medal round, the cards being counted at lunch. They played foursomes in the afternoon and dinner began between 5 p.m. and 6.30 depending on which train the town members had to catch.

Sheep's Head and Haggis

The Minutes tell how the town members made sure the decanters were empty before they departed. One delightful Minute recorded in 1888 shows the flavour of the East Lothian Golf Club. It requested the landlord of the Golf Hotel "to provide sheepshead and haggis at the next meeting and also to have his whisky and sherry in decanters not quite so like each other as, after a certain period of the evening, some of the members found it very difficult to distinguish which was which."

In 1892 the Secretary records "luncheon consisted of 10 dozen sandwiches from the Bodega and unlimited drinks. The day being very hot, a great deal more whisky, potash (soda) and beer was consumed than usual and the day was somewhat expensive but most enjoyable and everyone in good form (at dinner not at golf)".

Those convivial and civilised meetings continued until 1914 as the following extracts from the Minutes show:

"Gullane, 14th March, 1896. The Spring Meeting was held here today in fine weather. There was not a large turnout of members but all who were there, were of the very best. On comparing cards at lunch, it was found that the prize presented by Mr. Thomas Usher had been won by his old friend, Mr. Thomas Aitchison. A result which gave the greatest pleasure to the donor and to the Club generally.

The members dined together at 4.45 and a most enjoyable evening was spent. The President, Mr Andrew Usher, occupied the chair and presented the prize, a magnificent wine jug to Mr Aitchison, remarking on his renewal of youth and improved game. Mr. Aitchison was evidently so pleased with the prize, the honour of winning it and the way his victory was received, that he volunteered to present a prize, to be competed for at the Archerfield meeting in July.

Excellent songs were sung and many toasts were proposed and drunk with enthusiasm and it was with much difficulty that the Secretary got accounts squared up and the town members bundled into the trap for Drem.

The drive to Drem was enlivened by many humorous songs from Mr. John Innes, the other members joining heartily in the choruses to the delight and astonishment of the rural population. On reaching Drem, the members were so enamoured of their own company that they refused to be separated, and travelled to Edinburgh twelve in a compartment arranged for six. Cards and songs and numerous jokes made the usually tedious journey to Edinburgh pass as if in no time."

"A Fine Shot!" by John R. Barclay.

"23rd October, 1898. Gullane, Golf Hotel. A more delightful dinner the East Lothian never had. Song and speech and chaff and fun of all kind was the order of the day. For the first time the town members left by the new Gullane train. The country members melted away gradually."

Morning Toddy

"26th March, 1899. Gullane, Golf Hotel. The Spring Meeting was held here today but no golf was played. Snow began to fall at breakfast time and continued, so when we arrived at Gullane station we found it about four inches deep. Members disconsolately adjourned to the Golf Hotel to hold a council of war. They were not long disconsolate, however, for they found Mr. Nicholson of Saltcoats, with admirable forethought, had ordered on an extra big fire in the parlour and a copious supply of whisky and hot water. Toddy at 10.30 a.m. is not a usual beverage but after a little coaxing by Mr. Nicholson, the other members tried it and were surprised to find how much less whisky there is in a bottle when it is made into toddy than when used with cold water.

The greenkeeper, after partaking of the club's hospitality, bravely offered to sweep the first and last tees and greens. As the snow was now about six inches deep, this sporting offer had to be declined. It was decided to dine at lunch-time and play nap till then. This programme was carried out with great success; the town members returning to Edinburgh by the afternoon train well primed to withstand the cold by good solid and liquid refreshment."

"3rd November, 1901. Gullane. There was a large turnout of members but only 14 handed in cards and some of these were very bad. The Secretary (St. Clair Cunningham) regrets that although there is no doubt the Club is flourishing in every other way, it seems to be deteriorating in respect of the golf of its members."

Wind and Snow

"5th November, 1905. To avoid an early start on Saturday, the Secretary drove over on Friday night from Hedderwick Hill. He started about 4 o'clock but had not gone far before the most damnable storm of wind and snow and sleet and hail and rain arose that it had ever been his experience to face. The darkness was awful and even with a very fast horse, it took him over two hours to reach Gullane, absolutely soaked and benumbed, with water sloshing about in the dog-cart more like a boat at sea, and clubs and kit-bag all to pulp. However, a warm welcome, a fine fire and a hot toddy soon put all right.

Next morning the weather was A1 and after a most glorious round in warm winter sun, the members joined at the luncheon table. Foursomes in the afternoon and the most jovial dinner followed an excellent day's golf. Toasts and replies, not to mention songs, made time pass so quickly that it was with the utmost difficulty that the town members caught the train. Country members as usual did not hurry away but remained to see that so good an opportunity for continuing a pleasant evening was not lost."

Gullane Old Clubhouse.

Like all successful clubs, they were blessed with a series of splendid secretaries who gave their time and thought so that the members could enjoy their meetings. The club continued to enjoy its games and gatherings up until 1914 when "all meetings were allowed to lapse" and it was not until November 1919 that the medals were next played for.

The 1920s brought about a change in the pattern of the day's play. Lunch was now the important meal of the day, the evening meal did not survive the First World War. But the lunches were jolly and prolonged, one of the finest being the 75th meeting of the Club.

"The weather was perfectly hellish owing to a gale and a blizzard of rain. The members cheerfully battled their way round No. 3 and returned with sharpened appetites to do full justice to the excellent fare. Foursomes were arranged for the afternoon. The weather showed no improvement and most matches were decided over a shortened course. A convivial spirit was maintained, songs were being sung with rousing choruses. Each member, there were 20, drank well but wisely. The consumption for the day being 9 bottles of whisky, 3 bottles of Kummel and 2 bottles of sloe-gin, which might be considered moderate on such a day."

Genial and Noble

There was a gap during World War Two between June, 1939 and June, 1946, but the Club was soon back in full swing. The courses at Hedderwick Hill and Archerfield had both disappeared. Petrol rationing did not prevent a large outing on Gullane No. 3 in April '48. The 1949 Autumn Meeting was voted "a huge success despite the price of whisky".

The April Meeting in 1950 followed the usual plan: Medal in the morning, sumptuous lunch and foursomes in the afternoon. "Despite whisky supplies being restricted to three bottles, all agreed it was as good and enjoyable a meeting as could have been desired."

The Centenary Dinner was held on 23rd October, 1959, and "most of the members regretted that they would be unable to attend the bi-centenary celebrations." Golf the next day "was a trifle slow in getting under way."

In 1963 Dick Broughton became the Secretary and he recorded the Minutes for 15 years in the best traditions of the Club with a fine balance of efficiency and humour.

The East Lothian Golf Club still meets three times a year and seems to comprise "all that is graceful, genial and noble in the good old game of golf."

"Two Golfers" by John R. Barclay.

4

DIRLETON CASTLE GOLF CLUB

Secretary and Landlord

Founded in 1854, this Club is the oldest in continuous existence at Gullane. "The members were mostly shopkeepers, working men and artisans from Dirleton and Gullane. The subscription was 2/6d per annum and their first green-keeper was paid ten shillings a year. They met for practice once a fortnight at Gullane and Dirleton (Archerfield) alternately."

The original members were Mr Robert Cole, Archerfield; Mr David Saunders, Archerfield; Mr Peter Cathie, Dirleton; Mr Henry Robertson, Gullane; Mr George H. Stevens, Gullane; and Mr John Halliwell, Gullane. They elected George Stevens secretary. As he was the landlord of the Golf Tavern (the large white house beside the No. 2 car park) they met there.

Smiddy and Pond

They adopted the rules of Tantallon Golf Club with certain amendments. In 1855 the committee inspected the ground and resolved to change the course. In September of that year "The Committee proceeded to inspect the green" and "remove the play from the holes at the church yard gate, the Table hole, the whin patch and the barn door and in their place to make the first hole at, or near, the Smiddy park gate, the second at the rabbit burrow and the third at the head of the pond. And they have added one down near the racecourse immediately next from the pump hole."

The pond can now be seen as a depression in front of the tee on the 1st hole of Gullane No. 1. The pump hole ran from the present second tee up the road where the tractors now go, to the top of the hill. The racecourse ran along the present third hole, so the new hole was further out on the links.

The evolution of the courses can only clearly be seen by studying the magnificent series of maps presented to the club by Mr Hall-Blyth and hung in the Gullane Golf Clubhouse.

Dirleton Castle was a golf club devoted to medal play and the scores were meticulously recorded. From their earliest days, they were a force in

East Lothian competitions. The growth of the club is illustrated by extracts from the minutes:

Toast and Song

In 1857 we read "Toast and song went on with energy and great good taste rising to a climax of hilarity". But in Ocober, 1858, they agree that 23 members be "struck off for not paying their subscriptions". In July, 1859, the three new members proposed are all described as "grooms" which shows how important the training of horses was in the district.

In the July meeting of 1860, one member must have hoodwinked the handicap committee. It was recorded: "The medal won by Mr. Joseph Murray. Actual 63, allowed 25, nominal 38." (There were 13 holes.)

October, 1861. The club dined at the Inn as usual and those who loved snuff were supplied from a snuffbox in the shape of an oyster shell of frosted silver, presented by Mr. Hanson on the occasion of his mare "Calleroo" winning the St. Leger this year".

In April, 1862, the Secretary "declined to record the play of Samuel Bunting on account of its inconsistency with his usual and recorded play". In the margin the Secretary reveals that his score was 117.

County Cup

In April, 1869, "The Club dined together in the Inn and spent a very pleasant evening in talking of old friends and old matches and arranging for new ones, not the least of which was the prospect of sending out a good team to compete for the Wemyss Cup." (Now called the County Cup.)

In 1871 the name of Murray appears again. The Murray family made at least part of their living on Gullane Hill. Whether they were rabbit trappers or tended sheep is not revealed but their trade may be the origin of the name of the fifth hole on No. 1 "Murray's Hill".

The minutes of 9th August, 1872, include the selection of a team to play in the Wemyss Cup "over the Saltcoats and West Gullane Links". In 1878 they are called the Luffness Links. In 1877 a committee was chosen "to act along with any similar committee that the East Lothian Golf Club may appoint for the purpose of employing an officer to keep the green in order and extend the same from 13 holes to 18 holes."

13th July, 1878, the Captain announced that Messrs Alexander Whittock and William Renton Clapperton had superintended and borne the expense of extending the course to fifteen holes.

The year 1879 is the first indication of match play. "Several matches were played but no record presented to be kept". Again in April, 1880, after the medal results, George Stevens records "this closed the

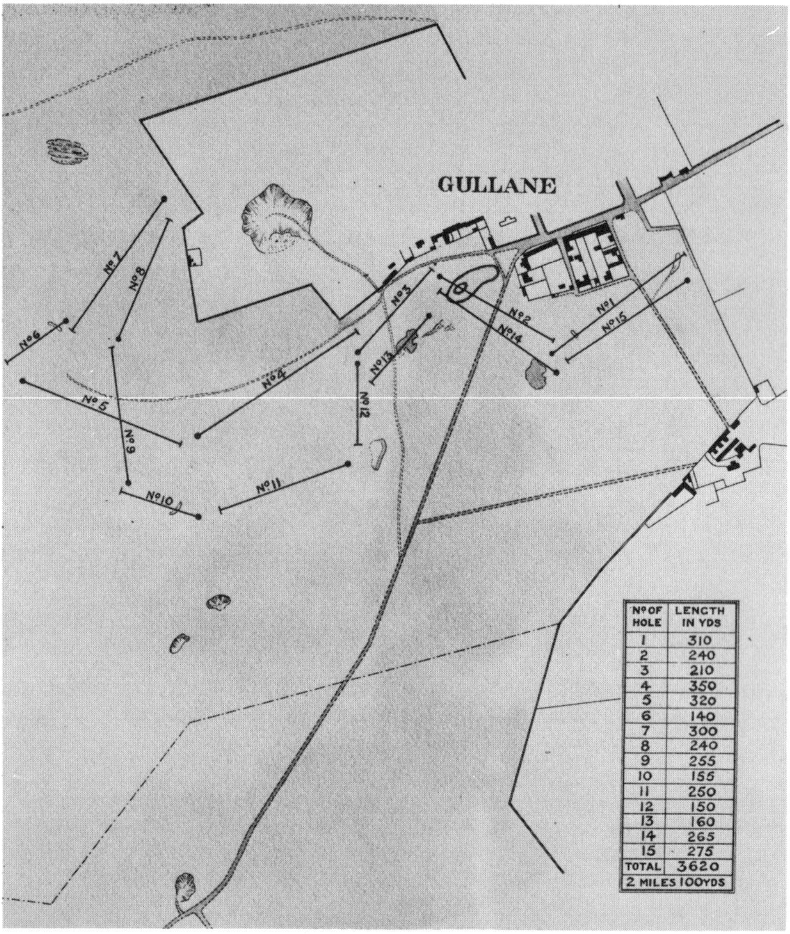

Map II shows the course starting and finishing in the Smiddy Park and going to the top of the hill.

competition but not the day's play of which no record was presented to me."

On the 29th July, 1882, the Rev. John Kerr of Dirleton was admitted as a member. He compiled the monumental "Golf Book of East Lothian" published in 1896.

In September, 1882, the committee "recommend to adopt and purchase the rules of the game as played by the Royal and Ancient Golf Club of St. Andrews."

Up to this time, the Dirleton Castle Club had used the Tantallon rules. In April, 1883, the Secretary reported "We have purchased 40 copies of the rules of the game as published by The Royal and Ancient Golf Club of St. Andrews at 6d per copy. The Secretary of the Royal Club writing that the cost to his club was 9d but they issued them at 6d to encourage their use generally".

Actual and Nominal

The Dirleton Castle Golf Club was now thriving, the numbers entering for each competition averaging 20. The minutes record all the scores, both "actual" and "nominal" and which prizes were won by each member. In September, 1883, there are four pages of beautiful handwriting recording those present; the new members; the scores and prizes of three rounds of golf! They conclude: "The Captain in handing over the prizes expressed his pleasure in the success of the winners and his hope that they would long be able to play as they had done today. The competition was from noon till 6 p.m., inlcuding half-an-hour for lunch."

In April, 1885, there was the last entry of George Stevens as secretary. He had been the driving force of Dirleton Castle for over 30 years. The Rev. John Kerr said: "Mr. Stevens was his Club's master; director-general of all its doing and concerns but the dictator was a good friend to the Club and at his death, left it in a healthy condition."

The Reverend gentleman was well able to judge because he acted as secretary/treasurer until a successor was found. There was now a period of calm at the club, and apart from the normal changes in office-bearers, only a few amusing or interesting minutes appear.

September, 1885: "Mr. A. Muir missed the train and the bus, and walked from Longniddry. He had been too late to play in the first round—could his score stand, and if so was it to stand in the first round or the second round?

After some discussion, it was decided to allow him to enter the second round. He tied for first place, but agreed to take second place, for which he won a brassie and six balls."

Handicaps were revised by the committee before every competition. Allowances were from scratch to 24, although very few received more than 12. Indeed after 1900 one or two men were given plus handicaps. In 1904 Hugh Cunningham recorded plus 6 and in March, 1906, won the monthly medal off plus-6, returning 76 plus 6 equals 82.

Match play was not often recorded but on the 6th September, 1888, match play handicapping "to be allowed on the first hole till the handicap runs out and in no case to be over one stroke a hole." Scores and results were always given, except on September 9th, 1893: "Unable to tell the name of the prize winners as one of the members took the results of the match into Edinburgh to put it in the newspaper and we never have found out who that member was."

A Ripple on the Pool

39th June, 1894: "A letter from the Secretary of Gullane Golf Club was read requesting the names and addresses of the members and it was unanimously agreed to take no notice." This is the only mention of the friction (which is detailed later) between the Dirleton Castle Golf Club and the Gullane Golf Club over the collection of visitors' green fees.

In September, 1895, the club was in a very prosperous condition with a balance of £7 6s. 4d. A donation of three guineas was sent to Gullane Golf Club towards the upkeep of the green but Gullane Golf Club sent it back. It was also resolved that the new members outside the parish should pay 7/6d entry fee and 5/- subscription. Parishioners were to pay only 5/- entry fee and 2/6d subscription.

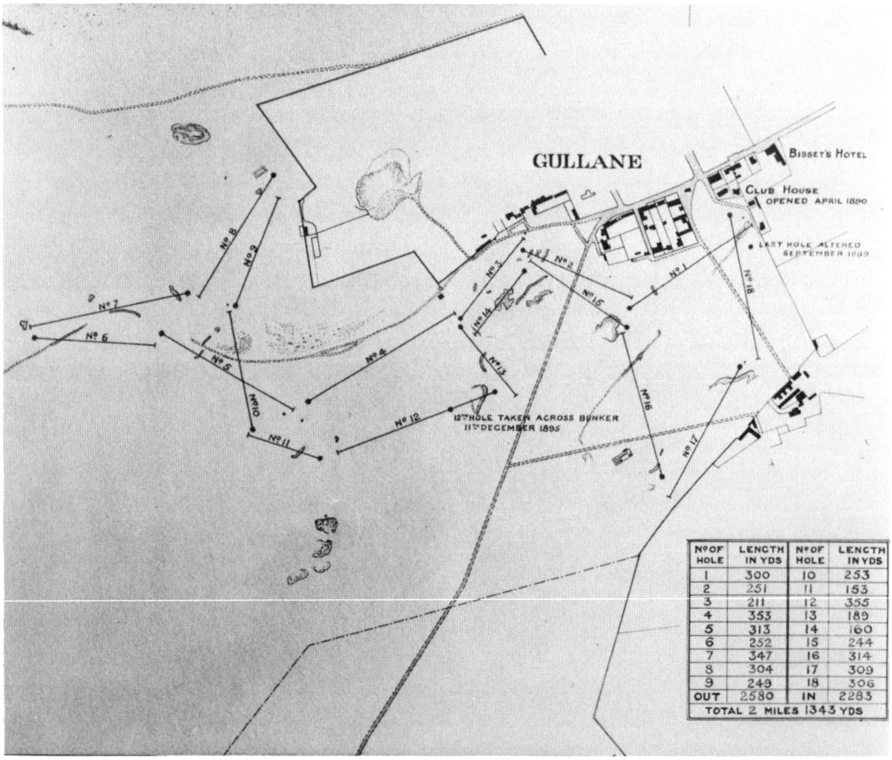

Nº OF HOLE	LENGTH IN YDS	Nº OF HOLE	LENGTH IN YDS
1	300	10	253
2	251	11	153
3	211	12	355
4	353	13	189
5	313	14	160
6	252	15	244
7	347	16	314
8	304	17	309
9	249	18	306
OUT	2580	IN	2283
TOTAL 2 MILES 1343 YDS			

Map III shows 18 holes.

Participation in the Wemyss (or County) Cup had been chronicled since 1864. The team was chosen by the committee, but the results were not recorded until 1899 when the secretary cut out a clipping from *The Scotsman* and pasted it in the minute book. This saved him a lot of writing. It records that, for the first time, the Cup was played on a course other than Old Luffness—i.e. Muirfield. It also records that Dirleton Castle Golf Club had won the competition for the first time in 13 years.

The Haldane Cup was another important trophy. It was an individual stroke-play tournament over two rounds, open to all East Lothian golfers, but at first supported largely by Direton Castle players.

Other interesting minutes include: August 15th, 1898: "The Secretary was instructed to write to those who were three years in arrears."

August 11th, 1904: "It was agreed to give £1 towards treating the Edinburgh Thistle Club to tea."

December 29th, 1904: "A committee meeting was held to appoint a secretary/treasurer, but as no one would accept the job, it was unanimously agreed for James Scott to take the work in hand for £3 per year for 1905, with a promise of a little more if the club raised the subscription at the end of the year."

Two Wins and a Loss

July 29th, 1907: County Cup at North Berwick. "Our team met the Gullane Club in the final and won at the 29th which was a close battle. Mr. Hall Blyth entertained all the players of the different clubs to dinner after the day's play at the New Club, North Berwick. Our team was: Mr. John Brotherston, Mr. Hugh Watt, Mr. William Black and Mr. James C. Kerr."

July 7th, 1908: "The Secretary was instructed to send 10/- towards the proposed memorial to Tom Morris, also to send for 100 penny new St. Andrews rules of golf."

July 24th, 1908: Wemyss Cup. "Our team beat the Bass Rock this morning 6 and 5, then beat New Luffness 5 and 4 this afternoon."

July 25th, 1908: "Beat Tantallon by 4 holes in the morning and in the final met New Club North Berwick and won by 4 and 3, which is a great victory for the Dirleton Castle Golf Club to win the County Cup for three years in succession over three greens, Kilspindie, North Berwick and New Gullane."

But next year their success declined: July 23rd, 1909: "The Dirleton Castle team got beat (sic) in first round of County Cup by Gullane Nine." If their success varied so did their expenses.

July 6th, 1910: "It was agreed to allow each player in the County Cup 25/- and, if put out on the first day's play, the second day's expenses deducted."

September 23rd, 1911: "Moved that no remuneration either cash or kind be awarded to players selected for County Cup matches played at home. Matches played away from home be awarded bona fide expenses paid by card."

August 13th, 1910: Haldane Cup. Hugh Watt returned the record score of 71. James Robertson Durham was second with 72.

September 14th, 1910. A letter was read from the secretary of the recreation room offering it as a club room at £2 per annum. It was accepted.

September 7th, 1914. It was proposed to put off the Patron's Medal and the Captain's Prize competition owing to the war. The next minute was not until February 5th, 1919, when the committee met to see if the club was to start play that season.

Two Stalwarts

Another splendid contribution to Dirleton Castle history has been made by Willie Gilchrist. He became secretary in 1924 and wrote all the minutes until October 1939 when, "It was decided to abandon all competitions during the war, and subscriptions to be voluntary". Fifteen years as secretary were only a part of Willie's life. He played "on the Hill" at every opportunity. He featured in an article written by the great golf writer Henry Longhurst who chose him to play in his eclectic team against the United States, as he had the best "life time ringer" score ever recorded. On No. 1 his best score at each hole reads an incredible 2, 2, 3, 2, 3, 2, 2, 2, 1 (19 out), 2, 2, 2, 1, 2, 3, 1, 2, 2 (17 back) total 36. Willie could be seen even in 1981, when he was 85, going out with a "spoon" to try to get an ace at the 4th. Sadly, late that year he suffered a stroke so that he can never sign a card better than level 2s.

A stalwart in the same mould is John Gordon, the present secretary. He took on the books and pen of office in October 1953, and so will soon begin his 30th year of unbroken service to this fine club. He is drawing close to the record set by Dirleton Castle's first secretary, the "Provost" of Gullane, George Heriot Stevens, who ran the club for 31 years. 27th April 1866, "the secretary called no meeting until May 1869 in consequence of the meagre attendance and having more pressing engagements."

His wife and children are secondary considerations.

5

GULLANE GOLF CLUB

Grass Very Rank

In August, 1882, eight gentlemen of Gullane met to consider the improvement and upkeep of the green which had been described in the East Lothian Club minutes of 1880 as "in very poor order. Mole hills being numerous and grass very rank." They were W. R. Clapperton, J. A. Molleson, G. McIntosh, J. C. Innes, G. H. Stevens, Thomas Lugton, Archibald Murray and John Watt. They resolved to form a club under the name of The Gullane Golf Club. Mr Clapperton was appointed President and Mr Lugton, Secretary. Messrs Clapperton and Molleson were instructed to draw up and issue a circular "To those golfers who were in the habit of playing over the links, with a view to inducing them to become members."

The circular was dated August 31st, 1882, and 32 names were given as members. The circular emphasised "the need for improving the green, the inadequacy of private subscriptions and the necessity of devoting a small but definite income to put the green in good order."

By September, 1882, the membership had reached 62. By 1883 when the limit of 100 was reached, it was raised to 125.

That year a gold medal was bought as the scratch trophy for £14. In 1884 the course was extended to 18 holes.

Manly and Intellectual

In 1889 subscriptions were invited to build a club-house and what is now called "The Old Clubhouse" was built and furnished for £500. Mr T. D. Thomson gave some lime trees which were planted round the clubhouse and he proposed that clubhouse and members be photographed. "The Courier" of the day commented: "A more manly and intellectual set of men no one need desire to look upon."

In September, 1891, a notice was put up at the 1st hole asking: "Golfers not members of the club to contribute towards the upkeep of the green."

In 1892 Thomas Lugton who had been Secretary from the club's inception, resigned. In 1893 the membership was increased to 300 and in 1894 raised to 400.

The income in 1895 was £543, the expenditure £319 and the balance in hand was now £562. The gutta-percha ball had saved the game of golf.

T. D. Thomson,
Captain 1884-1886.

Visitors were charged 1/- a day, 2/6d per month if they took a house in Gullane, 5/- a month if they stayed in a hotel. The annual ticket was 20/-, caddies were paid 1/- per round or 2/6d per day plus 6d for lunch.

Differences

In 1894 a disagreement arose between the Gullane Golf Club and Dirleton Castle. In order that the ranger could identify those entitled to play, the Gullane Club requested a list of members from Dirleton Castle and East Lothian golf clubs. The East Lothian Club submitted their list but Dirleton Castle declined without the consent of a general meeting of their club.

By August, the Gullane Club were proposing to withdraw the privilege of playing over the green free of charge. Mr A. B. Thomson, the Captain of Dirleton Castle, then wrote to the Secretary of Gullane Golf Club to say: "(1) That the Dirleton Castle Golf Club did not recognise the right of Lady Hamilton Ogilvie to let, rent or lease the right to play golf over Gullane Common. (2) That Dirleton Castle Golf Club agreed to help the Gullane Golf Club in the care of the green. (3) That they are pleased with the success of the Gullane Golf Club to improve the green and will take a more active hand in keeping the course up to the high standard it has now come to. (4) That they have arranged a tournament and invited other clubs to play at Gullane without paying as their guests."

On August 11th, 1894, the Gullane Golf Club committee then

resolved, with the approval of Mr and Mrs Hamilton Ogilvie, to withdraw the privilege granted to members of Dirleton Castle Golf Club of playing on the course free of charge, and informed the invited clubs of this decision. A month later, on September 13th, Dirleton Castle Golf Club offered three guineas donation towards the upkeep of the green. Gullane Golf Club decided to return this money.

Adjusted

Mr and Mrs Hamilton Ogilvie had suggested that another letter be sent to Dirleton Castle Golf Club affording them a further opportunity of giving a list of their members. Two days later, on September 15th, 1894, at the annual general meeting of the Gullane Golf Club, the Captain, Mr Turnbull, explained that the differences with the Dirleton Castle Golf Club had been adjusted. The Captain of Dirleton Castle Golf Club, Mr A. B. Thomson, "moved the thanks of the club to Mr Turnbull for his services as Captain of Gullane Golf Club for the past two years." The breach had been healed.

A New Course

The end of the 19th century approached with golf at Gullane booming. In 1898 a second, or relief, course was suggested. Willie Park junior was asked to look at the ground and direct the laying out of the new course. He came down from Musselburgh three times and went over the new course, giving his advice. He submitted an account for ten guineas. The committee of Gullane Club considered this excessive and directed the secretary to request Mr Park to modify his account. This Mr Park declined to do, so the amount was paid in full.

Willie Park Junior.

The Gullane Golf Club had organised, with the Ladies Golf Union in 1897, a ladies championship. It was a great success. The Club gave the ladies the use of the clubhouse while they asked the parish board to close the school during the competition so that the Club could have the use of it. This was agreed and the fee was ten guineas. "Bisset was allowed to put up a tent for cycles, at his own risk."

As 1900 approached, the railway opened Gullane station, with a corresponding increase in visitors. The Club had £900 in the bank. W. Logan was head greenkeeper and James Wilson secretary. Everything seemed perfect. Indeed the 15 years which led up to the First World War were smooth and successful. Only minor blemishes appeared and these were dispatched efficiently by a series of busy committees.

In 1905, the Club agreed with Mrs Hamilton Ogilvie, who owned most of Gullane, that present feuars could play golf on the old course free of charge and that any new feuars could pay half-charges. In 1908, a new lease was negotiated for the two existing courses and a lease made out for the third course which was being planned. The rent was to be £200 for 1908, rising to £300 by 1918. Members now paid a three guinea entry fee and two guineas annual subscription.

No. 3 for £1,000

The 1909 accounts show green fees of £1,000 and the cost of constructing the new course at just over £1,000. This year was also notable for the retiral of the Secretary, James Wilson. He had succeeded Thomas Lugton in 1892. To these two men Gullane Golf Club owed their splendid and solid start.

In 1910, Mr Hall Blyth presented the splendid set of maps which show the growth of the three courses and are an unique record of 27 years' progress.

Inflation!

September 3rd, 1912: the price of lager up from 3d to 4d and whisky and soda up from 5½d to 6d.

June 6th, 1913, it was decided not to insure the greens against raids or damage by suffragettes, but later the clubhouse was insured for £1,000 against both aircraft and bombardment.

New Clubhouse

In 1913, there was the first mention of a new clubhouse. A member offered to lend up to £10,000 at 5%. For some extraordinary reason, this offer was allowed to lapse and it was to be 14 years before the new clubhouse project was revived.

In June, 1914, the price of lunch was raised from 1/- to 2/-.

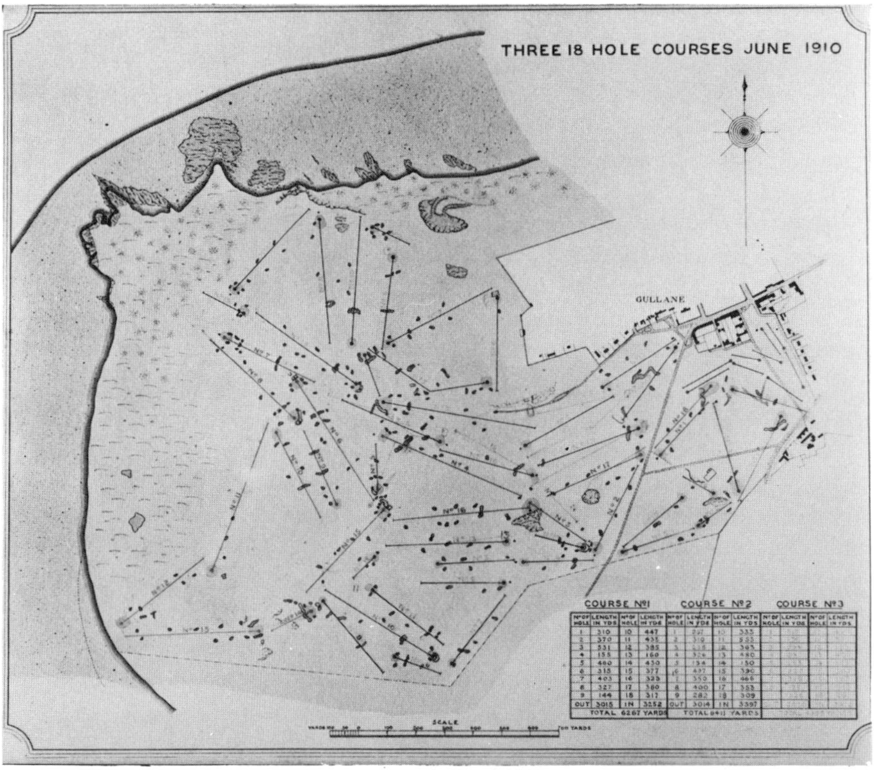

Map IV—three 18-hole courses, 1910.

Half Wages

In September, 1914, the committee decided to pay, for the duration of the war, half wages to eight members of the green staff now serving with the Colours. But they under-estimated the duration of the war and the decision was cancelled in 1915.

Sheep and no Water

In 1915, sheep were being grazed on the courses "earlier than usual, in very large numbers and with little or no supervision" and the committee decided that no greens should be watered.

Two Green Staff

In February, 1917, "Logan and Russell volunteered for national service, so that left only two green staff. The committee decided to carry on with two men only."

Six Strike

May 11th, 1920. The Secretary reported that six of the green staff had struck work that morning on account of dissatisfaction with the wages. They were granted another 5/- a week.

Lloyd George

August, 1920. Mr. R. W. Stevenson submitted a list of names for the holes on the No. 1 course. They were all approved, except for the 10th hole which he had called "Lloyd George".

Sunday Golf

November, 1924. The club conducted a plebiscite on Sunday golf, to be confined to Nos. 2 and 3 courses, limited to Gullane Golf Club members and their guests, Gullane Ladies Golf Club, Dirleton Castle Golf Club and Dirleton Castle Ladies Golf Club. 730 letters were sent out. There were 538 replies.

In favour of Sunday golf:	members 180,	housholders 90
against :	members 105,	householders 156.

Seven replies were neutral. The committee took no action.

Women Weeders

February, 1925: "On account of the urgent necessity of keeping down weeds on the green, two women have been appointed to the green staff."—a minute which revives memories of the 1930s, when women were to be seen on their knees weeding the greens while wearing their traditional East Lothian bonnets.

Light Relief

April, 1926. "It was reported that electric light had now been installed and it was decided to extend the light to the water closets."

Derby Cup

September, 1926. "Lord Derby wished to present a cup for a competition in which Gullane Golf Club and Dirleton Castle Golf Club should participate on equal terms."

Offer to Sell Courses

In October, 1936, Lieut.-Col. J. P. Nisbet Hamilton Grant, D.S.O., of Belhaven and Dirleton, who now owned the land on which the courses lay, offered to sell it for £5,920. The Committee asked about a price to include an extension to Gullane Point but no reply was recorded. The

A. W. Robertson Durham, Lord Derby and Major Smith (Secy.).

only comment in the minutes on the offer was a faint pencil note in the margin "More or less cancelled". A new lease was then agreed.

The lack of solid interest in the offer might have been due to the other important project ahead—the new clubhouse.

In six months, negotiations had proceeded steadily with only minor ripples. For example: June, 1927: "It was decided that the idea of a combined clubhouse (with Gullane Ladies Golf Club) was not feasible." This decision was happily reversed.

New Clubhouse

Lands surrounding the Gullane Ladies' clubhouse were acquired in the summer of 1927. Later that year, at the A.G.M., members approved plans to design and obtain tenders. A decision to build the new clubhouse followed.

The cost was covered by debentures from the members and by increasing entrance subscriptions from five guineas to seven guineas. A contract, still in operation, was made with Gullane Ladies' Golf Club, outlining the responsibilities and finances of the new clubhouse.

In the late spring of 1928, the old buildings on the site were demolished and in the autumn, construction work started. Among the innovations was the installation of electric light. This was quite advanced as only 18 months previously the Gullane Golf Club committee had approved funds for "fitting of an additonal gas bracket in the smoke room."

The new clubhouse was formally opened on December 20th, 1929, by the Captain of Gullane Ladies Golf Club, Mrs S. G. Rome.

Purchase of Courses

After the talks of 1926 on buying the courses had slowed to a halt, writing off the cost of the new clubhouse was a priority but by the autumn of 1932 the committee was again looking very seriously into the feasibility of purchase. Eventually all points were clarified.

On March 27th, 1933, at an Extraordinary General Meeting in Dowells Rooms, George Street, Edinburgh (the membership was predominantly resident in Edinburgh in those days) motions were unanimously approved to:

(1) Buy the three courses and the children's course for £7,380 from Colonel Grant.

(2) Borrow £5,000 to be repaid over 15 to 20 years and raise the balance by debentures from the members at an appropriate interest rate.

Apart from the obvious rights to control the playing of golf, the benefits included a share in crops measured in bushels and pecks from the feuars of small farmlands fringing the courses. There was also £60 a year from a rabbit trapper for the sole right to snare and ferret. Before World War II the rabbit featured prominently in the diet in Scotland. The £60 fee of 1933 for the right to trap rabbits would be worth more than £2,000 fifty years later.

The Thirties

With the new clubhouse the 1930s opened on a confident note. The Captain, Mr Hall-Blyth, invited the committee and their wives to lunch, along with the Captain and committee of Gullane Ladies Golf Club and past-Captains of both clubs, plus wives and husbands. The new dining-room was to be well-filled.

Everything seemed to be under control except Mrs Gray Muir's poultry: January 24th, 1930, "The Hon. Secretary was instructed to point out to Mrs. Gray Muir that so far the person in charge of her hens would appear to have received no instructions to prevent the hens doing damage to the grass in front of the Clubhouse."

East Links, Gullane—"Hens in the Bunker."

Gifts and Scores

May 9th, 1930—Mr. G. Franklin Smith gave the Club the cabinet containing the valuable collection of golf balls. Mr. W. D. Shaw gave the picture of Gullane Links by T. S. Nisbet.

November 14th, 1930—Lord Derby gave the Club the annual interest on his debentures. Mr. Freak-Palmer presented a clock. Mr. Jack White gave a picture of Sir John Nisbet of Dirleton. The Secretary, Major Smith, presented a barometer.

September 21st, 1931—Mr. Freak-Palmer presented a barograph.

November 25th, 1933—Lord Derby gave the bronze horse to mark the winning of three St. Legers, while staying at Gullane; Tranquil 1922, Fairway 1928 and Hyperion 1933.

While these handsome and generous gifts were enhancing the clubhouse, golf on the hill was also of a high standard. W. B. Torrance was playing off plus 2; C. Mann and J. C. Rose were plus 1. In the 1933 Summer Meeting, Tom Hay set a new record on No. 1 of 71. In the Haldane Cup in August, R. Ritchie of Dirleton Castle Golf Club set a new record on No. 2 of 68. At the Summer Meeting in 1934 R. A. M'Kinna equalled the record of both No. 1 and No. 2—71 and 68.

Sell the Horse

The scrap books record the scores and the winners of the 1930s but the euphoria is ended by the war. The minute of September 24th, 1939, runs: "Owing to the war, the green staff to be reduced to W. Logan, Head Greenkeeper and nine men, including two starters and a caddymaster, three girls and a rabbit-trapper; the three courses to be open for play on a care and maintenance basis. It was decided to sell the Clydesdale horse."

James Dishington, Greenkeeper.

The early 40s were years of adapting to the effects of the war. August 4th, 1940: "Alex Aitken, the club-maker, writes to say his takings are practically nil and requests that he should occupy the club-maker's shop rent free. This was agreed."

13th December, 1940: "Members serving with H.M. Forces should pay two guineas per annum."

March 1941: It was reported that a siren had been erected on the clubhouse and Air Raid Precautions had undertaken to keep the club free of all cost in connection with the erection, maintenance and dismantling of the siren.

Bullets, Bombs and Blocks

10th October, 1941: "The petrol allowance for the tractor has been cut down to 20 units for two months and with the short staff, the greenkeeper finds it impossible to keep up No. 3 course and asks that it be closed altogether. It was decided to ask Logan to endeavour to maintain the greens of No. 3. It was reported that the Home Guard were keeping stores in the clubhouse including ammunition and that access to the Secretary's cupboard was difficult."

24th January, 1943: A letter was read from the Air Officer commanding Drem, requesting the use of the ground between Aberlady Bay and the No. 1 and 2 courses, as an air target. It was agreed to allow this, subject to suitable arrangements being made to give warning when the range was to be used.

2nd March, 1945: "Mr. J. W. Gibb asked if there was any hope of having the concrete blocks removed from the 12th hole before the end of the war. The Captain, Mr. Hall-Blyth said the alternatives were: (1) burying the blocks, (2) blowing them up and (3) breaking them up and carting them away."

He reported that 200 German prisoners were available for the work.

16th September, 1945: The Captain reported that all anti-tank blocks which interfered with play at the 12th and 13th holes on No. 1 and No. 2 courses, had been very satisfactorily buried by the prisoners. In all 9,000 man-hours had been worked, at no expense to the Club.

Water Colours and Whisky

February, 1946: Seven water-colours of the courses painted by Frank Wood were presented to the Club by Lady Bingham and her daughter. They represent a valuable and beautiful record of how the course looked in the 1930s. Frank Wood was a gifted artist and his pictures are much sought after.

On Sunday 6th October, 1946, an emergency meeting of the Committee was called to consider the shortage of whisky and gin. An offer had been made by a firm of whisky merchants. It was decided to buy six cases each of whisky and gin and 72 gallons of whisky on the same terms as last year.

An approach was also to be made to all regular sources of supply for a special allotment of whisky and gin for the Ladies Amateur Championship.

"No member may on any one day order more than two small whiskies and two small gins for himself and his guests."

Silver and Balls

13th April, 1947: It was reported that the cornucopia silver horn trophy originally presented to the Hanky Panky golfers by Mr. W. R. Clapperton (first Captain of Gullane) had been given to the Club.

The reigning Captain, Ian Bowhill, gave a silver trophy for competition annually between the Gullane Golf Club and the Gullane Ladies Golf Club.

The Open Championship came to Muirfield in 1948 and Gullane was used as a qualifying course. The Captain reported that the Dunlop Company wanted to erect advertisements on the course near the main road during the Open Championship week of 1948. This was agreed if Dunlops would increase the quota of golf balls allocated to Ben Sayers for use of the Gullane Golf Club.

It was decided, along with Mr. Sayers, that one ball should be issued to each member through the Secretary. Of the 12 dozen, three dozen were to be allocated to Gullane Ladies Golf Club.

But it was later reported that Mr Sayers had not agreed. The balls had been handed over to him, he said and he had undertaken to sell them at 3/9d each singly to members in order of application.

23rd November, 1947: In view of the abolition of the basic petrol ration, it was suggested that a bus be hired to enable members to come to Gullane on Saturdays and Sundays. The fare was fixed at 5/- per head for the return journey, with a member entitled to bring one guest. However, the special bus ran only once. The police made enquiries and the Traffic Commissioner said that it should not continue because of the Road Traffic Act conditions.

The Fifties

Sheep had been grazed on Gullane Hill for many years but were affecting greenkeeping and in March, 1949, the Captain reported that Major Hope of Luffness Estate had agreed that grazing rights would end in March 1950.

The course was being continually improved in design at this time. Mr McKenzie Ross, the golf architect, produced a plan in 1949 which resulted in the improvement of the 14th, 15th and 16th holes.

In 1950 negotiations began to attract a professional to Gullane. Previously club-makers such as Alex Aitken, Jack White and Ben Sayers with various shops in the village, supplied clubs and balls but the Club now felt that a resident golf professional was needed and in the September Hugh Watt was appointed.

In February, 1951, seven water-colours were bequeathed to the Club

Alex Aitken's Shop.

by the 17th Earl of Derby. These water-colours by Anthony Raine-Barker now hang in the dining room.

August 1951: The Gullane team—G. W. Mackie (Captain), Guy Robertson-Durham and W. C. D. Hare won the Lothians Team Tournament with a score of 430. The Captain's individual contribution included a record 67 at Lothianburn and the Stewart Cup for the best individual aggregate.

In July, 1952, the brassie used by Bobby Jones in the Walker Cup Match at St Andrews in 1926 was presented by Mr Ian Bowhill and displayed in the smoking room.

The early 1950s saw the Club go through a difficult period. Petrol rationing reduced the membership and the visitors. Expenditure was very finely balanced with the income but by 1956 the worst was over. The subscription was eight guineas with no entry fee.

Fortunes Improve

The Club could boast many fine golfers at this time and in 1960 the Captain could congratulate the team on winning the County Cup for six years in succession. The team was drawn from G. W. Mackie, J. W. Draper, Peter Bryce, Dr C. R. D. Leeds, M. R. A. Matthews and R. H. J. Mackie.

In September, 1960, the green fees were fixed at: No. 1 for the day 10/-and at weekends for the day 15/-; No. 2, 7/6d a day and No. 3, 5/- a day.

In December 1961, the Club bought "Mayday" the house next to the Clubhouse and Mr Ronnie Balfour-Melville was appointed as Secretary.

He encouraged a high standard of behaviour within the Clubhouse and on the Hill. His eagle-eye spotted slow players on the three courses and they were soon encouraged to move more briskly.

The Club's fortunes continued to improve and by February, 1963, there were 82 waiting candidates, which represented a four-year wait for membership.

During the 1960s the Club made steady progress, the amenities of the Clubhouse were increased and the number of bunkers on the courses was reduced. The perennial complaints about slow play were received and dealt with, and the course steadily became busier. In 1969, 182 new members were admitted in the year.

One major improvement of the 60s, after ideas for a new larger clubhouse were dropped, was in the entrance hall. The new layout was also enhanced by twenty engravings by George Aikman of John Smart's paintings of the early golf greens of Scotland.

In 1972 the starter's wooden box was replaced but it was not the end of its life; it was moved down the road to be parked in the back garden of the starter, Jimmy Laidlaw!

Hugh Watt retired as professional in February, 1975. He had filled the post with a quiet dignity that impressed members and visitors. Sadly he died on the day of his presentation from the Club. His former assistant Jimmy Hume succeeded to the post to maintain the high standards of tuition and clubmaking.

The Match Dinners

The Club's Match Dinners, one of the happiest features of the Club, were suggested as far back as 1956 but no action was taken until Peter Bryce became Captain in 1963, when the first one was held. These agreeable evenings transformed the Club from a membership where many played in the same four every week to a congenial mixture of high and low handicappers.

At the dinners, foursomes are arranged on a handicap basis; the Recorder announces the matches with the stakes. The other diners join in with a gamble on their favourites.

Malcolm Matthews recorded from 1963 to 1970 when Dick Mackie took over. When Dick became Captain in 1974, he was succeeded by the genial Charlie Herd. 1978 was the first year of Gordon Smith, when the repartee became even sharper. The dinners became too numerous to be recorded by one scribe, so Mike Hutton became the Deputy Recorder and he and Gordon Smith combine their talents on alternate dinners.

A handsome lectern was presented in 1981 by Graeme Paul. This made it easier for the Recorder to see his list and the congregation at the same time.

The Match Dinners have been instrumental in cementing the membership of the Club into a warm and happy society. They have produced a Club without cliques; a large core of cordial and enthusiastic participants has improved the playing strength and Gullane competes vigorously and successfully in the Winter League and in matches against visiting Clubs.

REFLECTIONS.

HE : "Don't play golf! Don't you really? D'you know, I always think there's something funny about people who don't play golf!"

6

TOURNAMENTS AND CHAMPIONS

Charging admission fees at Gullane has never been attempted because of the easy access to the course but many of golf's best events have been held there.

The Scottish Ladies Championship has been played five times. In 1925 Miss J. Percy beat Miss Grant Suttie by two holes. In 1931 Miss J. McCullough beat Miss Doris Park at the 19th. In 1952 Miss Jean Donald beat Mrs R. T. Peel by 13 and 11. In 1964 Miss J. B. Lawrence beat Mrs S. M. Reid by 5 and 3 and in 1979 Miss G. Stewart beat Miss L. A. Hope by 2 and 1.

The Scottish Professional Championship was played in 1953 and won by Hector Thomson.

The Amateur Internationals were played in 1968 and the British Ladies Open Championship in 1897, 1947 and 1970 (won by Dinah Oxley).

Gullane was chosen as a qualifying course for the British Amateur in 1957 and for the Open in 1959 which was the year of Gary Player's win at Muirfield.

In 1966 and in 1972 the Open qualifying was on No. 1. Jack Nicklaus won in 1966; Lee Trevino won in 1972.

Golf, issuing from its narrow home in Scotland, has conquered the world.

In 1976 the British Youth's Championship was held over No. 1 when Sandy Lyle, later a successful tournament professional, was beaten in a play-off by Malcolm Lewis. In 1977, the Scottish Open Amateur Stroke Play Championship was held over Gullane and Muirfield. P. J. McKellar won with a score of 299. This was preceded by an amateur international match in which Scotland beat Spain over Gullane No. 1.

In 1980 both No. 1 and No. 2 courses were used as qualifying courses. The winner that year was Tom Watson. In 1981, the British Boys was played on Gullane No. 1 and the winner was Jesus Lopez of Spain.

R. Reid Jack.

The champions in Gullane Golf Club are led by R. Reid Jack. He was British Amateur Champion in 1957 and Scottish Amateur Champion in 1955. He played for Britain in the Walker Cup in 1957 and 1959. He was leading amateur in the Open Championship in 1959. He is closely followed by W. D. Smith who was Scottish Amateur Champion in 1958 and chosen for the Walker Cup in 1959. He was leading amateur in the Open Championship in 1957. Sandy Flockhart was the Scottish Amateur Champion in 1948. Sandy Williamson was British Boys Champion in 1939. In 1982 Alan Smith, a junior member, won the Scottish Boys Championship at Dunbar.

7

OTHER CLUBS

The Gullane Golfers

Formed in 1868 they were composed of well-known Edinburgh citizens with a liberal sprinkling of artists, including John Smart whose water colours were the inspiration for the engravings of "The Golf Greens of Scotland" now in the hall of Gullane Golf Club. They disbanded in 1903.

SCORE	1	2	3	4	5	6	7	8

The Gullane Golfers.

A Meeting on ______________ *Links,*

will be held on ______________

Train ______________

C. MORRISON, 34 St. Andrew Square.

Reply to Mr. ~~W. Paxton, Fountainhall Road~~, *before Tuesday.*

9	10	11	12	13	14	15	16	17	18	TOTAL

The Hanky Panky Golfers – 1871

These were mostly Bruntsfield members of high and congenial spirit: "No one was asked to join who sat at the wayside of life clad in sack cloth and ashes." Their name came from a jape played on one of their members whose clothes were strewn along the Drem railway station platform while he was in a "convenience". When he emerged, he shouted, "Who has played this hanky panky on me?" and the Club was named.

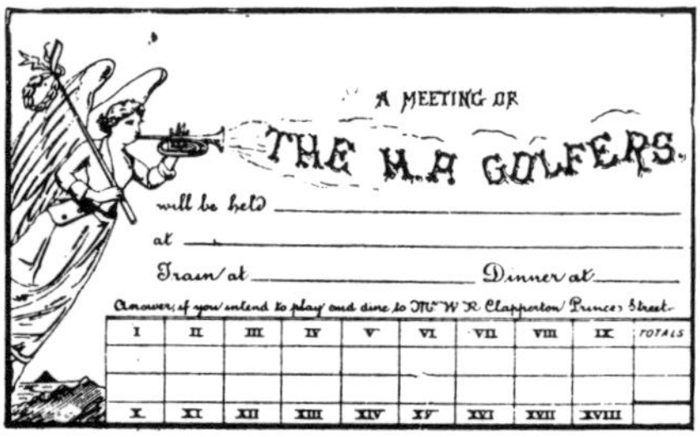

A MEETING OF

THE H.P. GOLFERS.

will be held ______________

at ______________

Train at ______________ Dinner at ______________

Answer, if you intend to play and dine to Mr. W. R. Clapperton Princes Street.

I	II	III	IV	V	VI	VII	VIII	IX	TOTALS
X	XI	XII	XIII	XIV	XV	XVI	XVII	XVIII	

The trophy which carries their name, was won three times, despite rigorous handicapping, by a Mr James Law and thus became his property. With the trophy gone they met only once or twice and faded from the golfing scene. But in 1981 the trophy was happily rediscovered under the stairs of Gullane Clubhouse and a mixed foursomes match-play tournament was very aptly arranged to compete for it.

THE ROUNDELL TEAM—WINNERS OF THE COUNTY CUP, 1891
(From a Photograph)

The Roundel Club

They met first in 1889 with their main object match play. The success of this policy was proved by the fact that they won the County Cup every time they entered for it! 1891 was the only occasion that they competed. They dined in the Roundel at the top of the hill.

The Harum Scarum Club

Formed before 1895, they played on the Queen's birthday. The winner had the privilege of inviting the members to supper after the event.

Gullane Nine Club

The first minutes were in 1896. They dealt with a golf competition on September 26th: After reporting the results, they deal with the purchase and the colour of a Club tie and the necessity to foster an "esprit de corps". Having achieved both objects, the Club quickly planned a dinner where speaking and singing were equally balanced, and lubricated by a good many toasts. Their golf meetings were usually in the autumn and their dinner in the New Year. The minute book contains the menu of each dinner. The selection of food makes the mouth water. The

Menu Card, Gullane Nine Club. J. D. H. McIntosh, Captain.

decoration of the menu card with photographs of the Captain now and in childhood, line drawings, crests and, inevitably, the motto "Forward" are a delight to the eye.

In February, 1900, the fare included broth, cod, beef, chicken and bacon, pudding and cheese. The occasion was a farewell to four of the members who were going to South Africa to serve in the Boer War. The minutes in May of that year announced that Mafeking had been relieved. Whether the first event had anything to do with the second is not revealed.

In April 1901 "the Gullane greens were very fast, one green being achieved in three by two players, who then took 8 and 10 respectively to hole out. Mr. Gebbie took 191 to hole the course. He did not think the greens were a fair test of golf."

In 1910 the Gullane Nine won the County Cup, the team being J. A. and A. W. Robertson-Durham, J. R. Stevenson and H. D. Lawrie. Despite this success, it is frequently pointed out to new members that the Gullane Nine is not a golf club but "A company of gentlemen inclined to golf".

If their golf was moderate, their rugby was splendid. "The Chairman congratulated Messrs Gillespie, Phipps-Turnbull and Flett on their caps in the English, Welsh and Irish Internationals and winning all three matches. In the Welsh match, the Gullane Nine Club did all the scoring and Mr. Gillespie had the honour of scoring the first try in each match."

The emphasis on song in the 19th century gave way to stories of varying degrees of vulgarity. There was also a good deal of horse-play and an annual attempt, often successful, to ring the village church bell after dinner.

The stories and the behaviour improved with the advance of the 20th century but alas, to date, the County Cup has not returned to the table of the Gullane Nine. Donald McIntosh was appointed secretary in 1948 and his enthusiasm contributed considerably to the health and strength of the Club.

Gullane Comrades

This club, formed in 1921, consisted of men who had served in the First World War and who were members of Dirleton Castle Golf Club or Gullane Golf Club. The object was to play golf. Social activity was confined to fund-raising whist drives. They played over Muirfield and Gullane Links and were able to field a strong team for the County Cup and the Evening Times Trophy, even though their best players usually played for Dirleton Castle. "The Committee decided that Dirleton Castle had first choice in all cases, except for the Times Trophy, but that any player had the right to play for the Comrades if he so desired."

The club was only two years old in 1923 when the Evening Times held their trophy at Gullane. Dirleton Castle committee selected R. Himsworth and John Watt. The Comrades selected Tom Dobson (winner of the Scottish Amateur Championship later in 1925) and Hugh Watt. Great was the rejoicing in the Comrades hut (opposite the fire station) when their gallant pair won the trophy.

This success inspired a flush of generosity next year. September 24th: "The committee recommended that a liberal allowance be made to the team in view of the fact that Gleneagles was a most expensive place. The allowance should be train fare plus 5/- on day of arrival, plus 15/- for a

Hugh Watt, Gullane Comrades, winner with Tom Dobson of the "Evening Times" trophy, 1923.

day's practice, and 15/- a day until the team was defeated." However, there is a note, in pencil in the margin, "cancelled at general meeting 1925." The Club had spent all its reserve on this venture and had to send off its team the following year with a much tighter purse.

If money was short, their venues were generous. In 1928, with an annual subscription of 5/- they decided their 72-hole stroke play competition for the Derby Cup, over four separate courses; Gullane No. 1, No. 3, Muirfield and Gullane No. 2. This was truly value for money.

The years ticked past to 1939 with only Thomas Kerr lasting more than two or three years as secretary. The scores are recorded, the winners are named.

After World War II, the Club soon resumed and Robert Hunter began a long and rewarding stewardship as secretary of this fine club.

In 1964, Messrs Sid Davies, Vic Logan, Jim Inglis and Alex Walker won the County Cup at North Berwick. They beat Haddington 8 and 7 in the first round; Dirleton Castle at the 19th in the second round; North Berwick at the 20th in the semi-final and Gullane 6 and 5 in the final.

In 1971, the Comrades, under the captaincy of Tom Watt, marked their jubilee with a very happy dinner dance at the Queens Hotel, Gullane, and presented Bob Hunter with a set of woods. The celebration of the jubilee year was so agreeable that the club began, at the ripe old age of 50, to hold regular socials and dinner dances. Success soon followed: in 1973, 50 years after they won the Times Trophy, Jim and Donald Hope, with Alex and Harvey Walker won the Lothian Team Trophy at North Berwick with a total of 292. They won the County Cup at Kilspindie in 1975. The team was Alex Walker, David Doughty, Alastair Walker and Donald Hope. They beat Dirleton Castle in the final.

In 1978, Vic Logan and Jim Hope won the Daily Mail National Foursomes Competition and won it again in 1979, a remarkable achievement as the competition covered the entire British Isles.

Surgeons versus Physicians, March 1893.

Macpherson. Gillespie. Maclagan. Buist. Thomson. Boyd. S. Thomson. Noel Paton. R. Thin. Robertson. Dunlop. Carmichael. Juke. Haultain. P. A. Young. Ronaldson. Ballantyne.

8

GREENKEEPERS

20th June, 1863, *The Courier*, Haddington reporting on a match between East Lothian Club and Bruntsfield: "The green was in beautiful condition and the weather was all that could be desired".

Golf Book of East Lothian by John Kerr 1896: "The Gullane Golf Course may be the most delightful in the world. There is an elasticity and spring about the turf and, as for the greens, even with all the wear and tear, where will you find their equal?"

With a gull's feather to mark the hole and with the paths between the greens smoothed and widened by walking, the first steps in green-keeping at Gullane were made by the players. The links of Bruntsfield, Leith and Musselburgh were well grazed and trodden as were the original three or four holes at Gullane, but as the course extended up the hill, it was necessary to assist nature. The 1854 improvements must have been modest because the first greenkeeper was paid (by the Dirleton Castle Golf Club) 10/- per annum.

When the East Lothian Club was revived in 1859, it combined with Dirleton Castle to pay the greenkeeper £1 each and provide him with "a cutter". One Club bought iron flag stakes, the other purchased "worsted to make flags with".

In 1864 the two Clubs had the satisfaction of seeing the first County Tournament played over their course at Gullane. There were 13 holes until 1878, when Mr Whittock and Mr Clapperton added at their own expense two more holes. This generosity was not enough to prevent the course becoming unkempt. The fall in standards was due to the problem of getting the two Clubs to act together.

In 1882 the Gullane Golf Club was founded because of the deterioration. A letter sent to those who played over Gullane showed this:

"Gullane Golf Club, Gullane, 31st August 1882.

Sir,

A meeting of proprietors and residents in Gullane was recently held with reference to the improving and keeping in order the golfing green. The result was the formation of a Club under the above name. The green has hitherto been kept in order almost exclusively by means of private subscriptions from summer visitors, but this has been found inadequate for the purpose while the soliciting of subscriptions is irksome and unpleasant.

A moderate outlay and a small but definite income will suffice to put the green in good order and maintain it efficiently. It is the intention of the Club to devote their funds, in the first instance, to the improvement of the green but any surplus may be expended on prizes to be competed for by the members, from time to time. It is also proposed that the membership should be limited in number but it is not yet determined what the limit should be.

The annual subscription has been fixed at 10/6d and the names of those gentlemen who have already joined the Club are appended hereto. Should you desire to become a member of the Club, I shall be much obliged by your filling up and returning the enclosed slip with remittance to the Hon. Secrerary, Mr. Thomas Lugton, Gullane, who will duly acknowledge receipt of the same.

In order that the Club may be put in working order before the close of the season, I shall be obliged by your doing this at your earliest convenience. If any of your friends should feel desirous of joining the Club I should be glad if you would send their names and address also to Mr. Lugton.

(signed) W. R. Clapperton
President.

W. R. Clapperton,
Captain, 1882-1884.

This was widely responded to and in September the membership reached 62.

George Shepherd was appointed the first greenkeeper on the following terms: October—8 days; November, December, January and February—4 days each; March—8 days; April and May—12 days each, at the rate of 3/- a day. A sum of £8 10s. was voted for this.

Extending the course was an early priority and only two years after the foundation of the Club the course was stretched in 1884 to the now-standard 18 holes.

Shepherd, the greenkeeper, for some time kept both Luffness and Gullane courses but in 1889, Luffness course lured him away and took his services "all to itself." So the Gullane Club appointed Alex Litster to work five days a week at 3/- a day. In 12 years—by 1894—the membership had jumped to 400 and the greenkeeper now spent his whole time on the green at 30/- a week and did his work so well that the Gullane greens were said to be admired by all comers.

There was also appointed, at this time, a ground officer at 28/- a week who collected subscriptions from people playing over the links who were not members of any of the privileged clubs. He also assisted the greenkeeper.

By 1898, the course was so busy that a relief course was planned. Willie Park advised about its layout.

In 1910, the No. 3 course was added and Gullane Hill, if Luffness is included, now had 72 holes of fine links golf.

Early this century Willie Logan began his long career as head greenkeeper. His reign lasted over 40 years and the courses flourished under his industrious and skilful hands. He knew the flora of the hill and made a definitive collection of the grasses which grew on Gullane Hill. They were identified and displayed by Suttons, the grass seed firm and an authority on links grass.

Logan also supervised the making of the present second hole on No. 1. The old hole ran up the hill (see Michael Brown's picture) and Lord Derby on his holiday visits to Gullane liked it less every year. In 1934 he left £400 with the secretary to have it changed.

There were two problems. A small stream ran down the valley and, close to the burn, was a right of way. Logan put the water into pipes and diverted the path up the right hand hill. With 15 horses he scooped the top of the left hand hill into the valley to make the hole as it is today. In its early days the hole was known as "Easy Going" (see Michael Brown on page 54). Willie Logan's son was later to be head greenkeeper at Muirfield and earn the M.B.E. for his services to golf.

The only other hole to be materially altered in recent years was the 12th on No. 2.

Bernard Darwin, the best of all golf writers, said: "It was a particularly fascinating hole, not so much for its intrinsic merits as for its secrecy and picturesqueness. While we are playing the holes before it, we become aware of it lying below us, very solitary and as if it belonged to nobody. Then quite suddenly we find ourselves driving to it. Beyond it lie nothing but sand hills and surf, and all the other golfers are hidden behind us. We feel as if we are playing in a little world of our own; our's and the gulls' and the rabbits'."

This hole was redesigned in 1970 under the supervision of Andrew Anderson who was head greenkeeper from 1954 to 1974. These were the difficult years after the war and the courses are a great credit to his skill.

Tom O'Brien came from Ratho in 1974 and his industry and ability were so obvious that by 1978 he was lured away by Royal Birkdale.

Tom Watt, brother of Hugh Watt, became head greenkeeper and the high standard was maintained despite the heavy traffic of visitors—the Club welcomes over 20,000 visitors every year.

Unlike many club golfers, Gullane members play the ball as it lies all winter, with no preferred lies and winter greens are seldom used.

"A Difficult Lie?" by John R. Barclay.

9

THE LADIES

Dancing and Tea

The Farmers Club—or to give their full title, the East Lothian Golf Club— from early in their annals, welcomed ladies to the links, not to play golf but to have lunch, to dance and to have tea in a tent near the hill-top.

August 3rd, 1860: *The Courier* records such a gathering, saying that the new Club was following the custom of the old Club (another clue that the Club had existed before 1859). "The president wishes the new Club to follow in the footsteps of the old one who often gave their lady friends an opportunity of sharing in those open air amusements which are too generally confined to the gentlemen. The picnic was a very happy one, the dinner in the tent a great feature and the keen air of Gullane Hill seemed to have sharpened all appetites. After dinner, we had two hours dancing, after which came tea, a luxury which the ladies seemed particularly to enjoy."

British Ladies 1897

After than entry, the mention of ladies is very scarce but an occasional member complains by letter to the committee that "the course is too much congested with ladies and children." This attitude must have been rare because, with the Ladies Golf Union, the Gullane Golf Club organised in 1897 the British Ladies Championship (see Michael Brown picture) and hospitably handed over the clubhouse to the ladies while members used the parish board school. There was a record entry of 102 competitors, one from Wales, 10 from Ireland, 38 Scots and the rest from England.

The quality of the Scottish ladies' play was a revelation to everyone because they had not appeared at any of the previous four venues; 1893—St. Anne's; 1894—Littleston; 1895—Portrush and 1896—Hoylake. Only one English lady reached the 4th round, Miss Neville. The semi-finals were between Miss E. C. Orr and Miss Titterton and between Miss Orr and Miss Kennedy. The sisters met in the final when the younger one, Miss E. C. Orr won by 4 and 2.

The British Ladies' Championship was not to return to Gullane for 50 years when the great "Babe" (Mildred) Zaharias strode the hill as one of its most memorable competitors.

Between these two events, ladies' golf was to change completely. In

1904, 14 ladies met in Dowell's Rooms, Edinburgh to form the Gullane Ladies Golf Club. 33 others had intimated their intention to join. They leased a room in George Leishman's house "Marionville" for £6 but this only lasted a year. They then rented a wooden clubhouse from Alex Aitken, the club maker, for £5 per annum and spent £12 15s. on fitting a lavatory.

In 1911 they agreed with Gullane Golf Club to compound the Clubs. They moved to the Gullane Reading Club but arranged to uplift the lavatory from the wooden hut.

In October, 1920, they obtained a feu of "Shepherd's Cottage", next to "May Day", for £10 per annum. This was the first step in acquiring the land for the present clubhouse and showed the astuteness of the ladies. They added Lennox's house, an adjoining plot, in June 1921 so that they had a useful piece of land with which to negotiate with Gullane Golf Club in 1927 over the building of a joint clubhouse.

Ladies Championship 1947, Gullane

It was dominated by "Babe" Zaharias (pronounced Za-Harris). She had, as Mildred Didrikson, won the Olympic Gold Medals for javelin and hurdles. She also broke the record for the high jump but was disqualified for using the "Western Roll".

"Babe" Zaharias,
British Ladies Champion, 1947.

British Ladies' Championship at Gullane, 1897, by Michael Brown.

1. Miss MACKINLAY, Dunbar.
2. Mrs DAVID CRAWFORD, Portobello.
3. W. RYDER RICHARDSON, Esq., Secretary, Royal Liverpool Golf Club, Hoylake.
4. Miss A. MAXWELL, North Berwick.
5. Miss N. GRAHAM, County Down.
6. Miss CARSON, Royal Belfast.
7. Miss DOD, Moreton.
8. Miss NEVILE, Worcestershire.
9. Miss ORR, North Berwick.
10. Miss MARY H. AITKEN, Falkirk Tryst.
11. Miss M, R. NIMMO, Falkirk Tryst.
12. Miss BLANCHE ANDERSON, North Berwick.
13. Miss E. C. ORR, N. Berwick *(Champion)*.
14. Miss MAUDE AITCHISON, Edinburgh.
15. Miss ISSETTE PEARSON, Wimbledon, Hon. Sec., Ladies' Golf Union.
16. J. TALBOT FAIR, Esq., Vice-President, Ladies' Golf Union.
17. Miss L. THOMSON, Wimbledon.
18. Miss E. M. TITTERTON, Portobello.
19. Miss PASCOE, Woking.
20. Miss K. MOELLER, Ilkley.
21. Miss A. L. ORR, North Berwick.
22. Miss E. L. KENNEDY, Rhyl.
23. J. S. WILSON, Esq., Hon. Sec., Gullane Golf Club.
24. T. H. MILLER, Esq., Singleton Park, Poulton-le-Fylde.
25. Mrs RYDER RICHARDSON, Hoylake.
26. Miss STARKIE BENCE, Royal Eastbourne.
27. Miss LILIAN SMITH, Minchinhampton.

Key to the picture by Michael Brown.

Mildred Didrikson was sixth of seven children born to Norwegian parents. They moved to Texas where "Babe" worked in a Dallas insurance company. After the 1932 Olympics she lost her amateur status in athletics—she dabbled in basketball, baseball and tennis. Then she saw Bobby Jones in an exhibition match and her desire to excel at golf was born.

She won a Houston tournament and was then told she was a professional and ineligible to compete in amateur events. She went on tour with Gene Sarazen and learnt a great deal from this charming and gifted man. She was tall, slim, straight and well balanced, but she was still an immature golfer and, although she played twice with Joyce Wethered she could not yet either match her scores or appreciate her timing and artistry.

In January 1938, she entered the Los Angeles Open where there was nothing to prevent a woman competing. She was paired with a professional wrestler, George Zaharias and they were married by December. She applied for amateur reinstatement in 1940 but had to wait three years by which time the war had put an end to all except charity matches.

It was 1946 before "Babe" won the National Amateur at Tulsa, Oklahoma and the Texas Open in 1947.

When she arrived at Gullane in June for the British Ladies Championship, the course was still unusually soft. This suited her style and strength, for she out-hit all her opponents. The quiet reserve of the galleries puzzled her but she never completely controlled her enthusiasm. She had watched the Home Internationals the week before the "Ladies" and was amazed at the restraint of the applause.

When the match play started, she progressed with impressive victories. In her six matches, she was twice taken to the 16th, otherwise she shook hands once on the 14th, the 13th twice and in the final at the 32nd. Jean Donald, who lost to her in the semi-final, said she was a delightful and sporting opponent and a popular champion.

Three thousand people watched the final and saw Jacqueline Gordon go two up after 11 holes, but by lunch they were all square—round in 75.

Miss Gordon lost the 19th, Babe had a 3 at the 20th and the die was cast. The power of her long game and the fiendish accuracy of her short game, were enough for her to win by 5 and 4. The British Ladies Trophy was to be carried off to the U.S.A. for the first time.

The Home Internationals which preceded the British Ladies, were won by Scotland, who beat Wales 9-0, Ireland 6-3 and England 7-2. This was the hey-day of Ladies golf at Gullane because in that victorious team were: the legendary Mrs Beddows, Doris Park, Katy Park and, of course, Jean Donald.

Jean Anderson (Donald).

Jean went one step better in 1948 at Lytham in the British Ladies and lost by one hole to Louise Suggs U.S.A. in the final. Jean stands well clear of any other lady golfer from these parts and, although she came from North Berwick and entered many competitions from there, she became more involved at Gullane as her career progressed.

The British Ladies Championship came back to Gullane in 1978, when Miss D. Oxley beat Mrs I. C. Robertson in a thrilling final by one hole.

Roll of Honour

The Gullane Ladies roll of honour is very impressive:

Fiona Anderson — winner Scottish Ladies 1987; runner-up 1980, 1983, 1988, 1991.

Mrs J. Anderson (Jean Donald) — runner-up British Ladies 1948; winner Scottish Ladies 1947, 1949 and 1952; runner-up Scottish Ladies 1953; Curtis Cup.

Mrs E. C. Beddows (Mrs Watson) — winner Scottish Ladies 1920, 1921, 1922 and 1929; runner-up 1923 and 1950; Curtis Cup.

Mrs M. L. Draper (Mrs Peel) — winner Scottish Ladies 1954; runner-up 1952 and 1962; Curtis Cup.

Mrs A. J. R. Ferguson (Marjory Fowler) — runner-up Scottish Ladies 1966 and 1971; Curtis Cup.

Lesley Hope — winner Scottish Ladies 1975; runner-up 1979 and 1986.

Catriona Lambert — winner Scottish Ladies 1991; Curtis Cup 1990 and 1992.

Connie Lugton — winner Scottish Ladies 1977; runner-up 1972.

Mrs D. MacIntosh (Barbara Dixon)—winner English Ladies 1969.

Mrs J. C. Milton (honorary member of Gullane Ladies)—winner British Ladies 1952; runner-up Scottish Ladies 1957; Curtis Cup.

Mrs A. Pickard (Miss Nichol)—winner of English Ladies 1960; runner-up 1957 and 1967; Curtis Cup.

Mrs A. Porter (Doris Park)—winner Scottish Ladies 1936; runner-up 1929, 1930 and 1931; runner-up British Ladies 1937; Curtis Cup.

Mrs W. C. Ritchie (Miss C. M. Park)—runner-up Scottish Ladies 1939.

The Ladies Club is lively and friendly. They can produce a very strong team and often defeat the Gullane Golf Club in the annual match for the Bowhill Trophy.

A well-fitting skiit.

10

VARIOUS PRAISE

Bernard Darwin called Gullane Hill "one of the most beautiful spots in the world."

Writing in *The Times* in 1934 he recalled "the sun shining and the wind blowing; the black clouds banked beyond the Forth and just a glimpse in the distance of the mighty tracery of the Forth Bridge.

The baby rabbits whisk their frightened little white tails in and out of the rough, the gulls pipe and the whole great stretch could engulf all the players and yet, especially towards the sea, lie wonderfully solitary.

Flags flutter and bunkers rear their sandy crests on every side and were it not for his caddy to direct him, he might start on Gullane No. 1, stray unknowingly on to No. 2 or No. 3 and find himself, in the end, on New Luffness. He could scarcely wander to Muirfield or Archerfield since they are a little cut off from the other four but they are but a metaphorical stone's throw away and have the same lovely turf that can put a little spring into the most leaden and depressed foot.

Save for the road along which the odious motors purr ceaselessly, it is divinely peaceful and lonely. Through the green the ball sits up waiting to be hit, on the greens it must be soothed rather than bludgeoned towards the hole.

Having played Gullane No. 2 in the morning and No. 1 in the afternoon, my mind is in an agreeable jumble between the two. There is, of course, a strong family likeness between the two because on both we have (like the Grand Old Duke of York of the poem) to march up to the top of the hill and march down again. The marching up at the second hole on No. 1 and the third hole on No. 2 is desperate work, but once we are at the top, the golf on both courses is most engaging and good sound golf as well. The marching down in each case to the 17th is good fun enough, involving a cheerful joy shot and the thought of a little refreshment."

Golfing Reminiscences: Mabel Stringer

"In 1897, we went to Scotland, the venue of the Ladies Championship being Gullane, one of the most famous of the many Lothian Links. We were all tremendously impressed by the play of the Scots ladies and we were sufficiently well versed in the game to realise that here we English golfers were quite outclassed. The natives were not very kind to us. They were most uncomplimentary about our beloved red coats. They made us pay the utmost farthing for everything. One day at tea in the school (which we used as a club) two or three of us chose a table in the window overlooking the links. When we were given our bill we found we had been charged nearly double the sum we had paid the preceding day and were told that the extra charge was for sitting in the window and "bang went a guid English saxpence."

The weather throughout the meeting was dreadful, our clothes were never dry and our smart stiff sailor hats were limp and misshapen. Our beautiful red jackets & showy garments, as the natives derisorily dubbed them, lost all their smartness and the whole time we were there we only had one really glorious day and that was the sabbath when we went on an excursion to Tantallon Castle. Next day we resumed the serious business of golf and were again given a salutory lesson in taking a back-seat graceful and sportingly, for three Scots lassies headed the stroke competition, Miss Orr, Miss Aitchison and Miss Annie Maxwell. We did not even win the small events such as driving and approaching for the former was won by a certain Miss Jarvie (a most appropriate name) from St Andrews with a carry of 133 yards. Day by day we southerners learned fresh lessons of humility as one by one our hopes were dashed."

Golfing Memories: Joyce Wethered

"Gullane has not yet lost the quaint and rural character of the first tee. The way of approach is down the village street. One steps straight off it, as it were, on to a village green, to tee up beneath the shade of the plane trees. But seldom is one allowed to linger. The sound of the bell and the voice of the starter summon the player to strike off and leave this pleasant spot. The holes lead one to the top of Gullane Hill, to unfold on every side a view famous throughout the land for its wonder and distance. Away up the firth can be seen Arthur's Seat rising above the smoke laden haze of Leith. To the south lie the Lammermuir Hills spread in a protecting belt which encloses a plain of corn and barley fields. To the east and north, the sea and the firth lie glimmering beneath us dotted with ships and islands; and over and across the water, the slopes of Fife fade peacefully into the distance.

I may be suspected of neglecting the golf too much for the scenery but how can one be indifferent where the beauty is so distracting.

The links of East Lothian speak for themselves, they need no advertising from members of the outside world. Everyone loves them and everyone revisits them."

The World of Golf: Garden Smith—1898

"Gullane Hill, untouched by the invading ploughshare, has left stretches of the most beautiful golfing country in the world. Turf of exceptional closeness and elasticity, natural sand bunkers of endless shape and variety, sierras of benty dunes and saharas of sand alternating with oases of verdure make the place a veritable golfers paradise. Here surely, if anywhere, must have been the home of our first golfing parents, for nowhere else in the world is the golfing prospect so expansive and enticing. Nowhere does the pursuit of the game seem so inevitable."

Andrew Lang—1884

I hae played in the frost and the thaw,
I hae played since the year '33,
I hae played in the rain and the snaw,
and I trust I may play till I dee.

A poem by John Thomson from the Golf Book of East Lothian—1896

It's up the hill and doon the hill,
And roond the hill and a' man;
And ye should come to Gullane Hill
If you can golf at a' man.
We'll cure you of a summer's cold
Or of a winter's cough,
We'll mak you young even though you're old,
So come and play at golf.

A poem by W. T. Hogg taken from "Golf"—1890

Folks praise the links beyond the Forth,
St. Andrews, Elie, Leven;
About Carnoustie, Dornoch Firth
Our ears they oft are deevin'.
But Gullane, Oh your wonderous charm
All other links surpasses;
Inspired we climb your hills as once
The ancients climbed Parnassus.

Horace Hutchison—Famous Golf Links 1891

"Gullane is a public green and inferior in merit. On the other hand, the walk round is a very pleasant one and it is justly famous for its putting green. By the artifice of man, it might be greatly improved but too much golf will ruin it. East Lothian turf is thin where ever it is true sea grass."

Sketches of East Lothian by D. Croall—1873

"Gullane leans towards the dry and sunny and the sun, though it does not often cause a man to tear off his clothes, sheds a singularly radiant light upon land and sea. Over the wide shiny sands of Aberlady Bay the far receding tides still race and in autumn push before them great companies of curlews, knots, dunlins and oyster catchers, of greenshanks and ducks, of plovers (grey and golden), and sandpipers. While from the fields at sunset, the wild geese come honking down to swell the nightly clamour of the shore."

The Game's Afoot—by Bernard Darwin, 1926

"If I could have the photograph I want to paste in my book it should not be of any group of players, but of the brown, grinning, resolute face of my caddy. This was a great little boy and it was a lucky chance by which I picked him up, one of the importunate throng in the streets of Gullane. He told me early in our acquaintance that he was one of the best caddies in Gullane and I do not quarrel with the description. He was very keen on the game and once, at a critical moment, broke into rapturous if subdued clapping. But he was still keener I think on birds and beasts, so that a round with him resembled, to borrow a famous title, a naturalist's voyage round the world. He dragged me far into the rough at Gullane to show me a plover's nest with eggs in it. Another time he found a lark's nest.

A little later he dashed away for a moment and reappeared holding a baby plover in each of his brown hands. I should add that he replaced them very tenderly whence they came."

Golf—The Badminton Edition 1890—Arthur Balfour

"A tolerable day, a tolerable green, a tolerable opponent supply, or ought to supply, all that any reasonably constituted human being should require in the way of entertainment. With a fine sea view and a clear course in front of him, the golfer may be excused if he regards golf, even though it be indifferent golf, as the true and adequate end of man's existence."

The Golfer's Guide 1894—Rev. John Kerr

"There is no quainter or more romantic spot than Gullane. Nor are there finer links anywhere; try them for yourself. And what with hill and valley, fresh air and fine scenery, say if you can bring me anything to match my beloved Gullane."

The Golf Courses of the British Isles—Bernard Darwin 1910

"There is probably no other golfing centre that is quite so good as Gullane. If the golfer can get up early enough in the morning and has the strength to do it, he can play seven courses on one long day."

British Golf Links 1897

The Gullane Links are a remarkable testimony to the usefulness of the much abused rabbit as a greenkeeper. It is to his agency that the turf owes its extraordinary springiness, enabling man to play golf from morn till dewy eve of the longest summer day without more than a proper and comfortable sense of fatigue."

W. D. Smith (Dick)—leading amateur Open Championship 1957, Scottish Amateur Champion 1958 and Walker Cup 1959.

"As I set off from Selkirk heading for the coast and Gullane, I have that pleasant feeling of anticipation which heightens as I crest the hill at the Haddington monument and the whole vista of the coastline comes into view with Gullane Hill standing out in sharp relief. Soon I am pulling off the main road into the attractive frontage of the clubhouse, then the magic moment when, with kindred spirits I step onto the first tee. This is ideally sited, initiating as it does, one of the few flat holes on the course. I think the main feature of No.1 must surely be its impressive slopes which make it virtually unique among links courses, that in the main tend to conform to sea level. Pride of place goes to the location of the 7th tee, providing the most magnificent panoramic view of the Firth of Forth which must be unsurpassed anywhere. For added value, there is a bird's eye view of the famous Muirfield course. Another prominent feature is the construction of the bunkers so as to give the errant ball little or no chance of running through them. The greens offer a constant challenge with their subtle contours and fast surface, often aided and abetted by the sea breezes. A round over No. 1 is always a satisfying experience and a good score is well earned."

Jean Anderson (Donald)—Scottish Ladies Champion, 1947, 1949, 1952, Curtis Cup

On a clear day there can be very few views as magnificent as the one from the 7th tee. From this tee one gets a complete panoramic picture. There can be few scenes more beautiful on an August evening than the sight from the 17th tee of the golden fields ready for harvesting to the south of the village.

It is at times difficult to concentrate on the golf, for combined with the magnificent scenery, one has to contend with the sound of the sky-larks and the peewits and the occasional raucous noise of a cock pheasant.

One is very conscious of the history of Gullane. So many people have played these links. I was privileged to play as long ago as 1946 in a foursome with James Braid, one of the great triumvirate. What an education that was! In that foursome was Mrs Charlotte Beddows, one of Gullane's most famous personalities. In 1947 I played with the amazing Babe Zaharias. These golfers are, alas, no longer with us but are a part of golfing history.

Sandy Williamson

"It is remarkable how little Gullane and the surrounding countryside has changed over the years. There is a feeling of peace and history few places have managed to retain. This is due to the large area of nature reserve adjoining the golf courses at Gullane Hill. I have never lost the enjoyment of reaching the 7th tee and of suddenly coming upon the vast panorama of sea, cultivated land and hills. The air is so pure and the space so vast that one experiences a great feeling of freedom. Golf becomes a relaxation and not just a matter of obtaining a good score. Where else can a golfer hit golf balls off superb turf surrounded by such a variety of scenery and wild life?

"Well Away" by John R. Barclay.

GULLANE GOLF CLUB CHAMPIONS

1950	G. Robertson Durham
1951	S. B. Williamson
1952	W. C. D. Hare
1953	G. W. Mackie
1954	D. O. Bergh
1955	S. B. Williamson
1956	G. Robertson Durham
1957	S. B. Williamson
1958	S. B. Williamson
1959	S. B. Williamson
1960	R. C. Napier
1961	S. B. Williamson
1962	S. B. Williamson
1963	D. R. Forrest
1964	S. B. Williamson
1965	S. B. Williamson
1966	J. E. Jackson
1967	R. Reid Jack
1968	R. P. White
1969	J. G. McGregor
1970	J. R. Inglis
1971	L. A. Gordon
1972	C. V. Murphy
1973	R. P. White
1974	L. A. Gordon
1975	R. Reid Jack
1976	R. Reid Jack
1977	L. A. Gordon
1978	J. R. Inglis
1979	J. R. Inglis
1980	J. R. Inglis
1981	J. R. Inglis
1982	J. E. Cook
1983	J. R. Inglis
1984	D. Doughty
1985	J. B. Dunlop
1986	J. T. C. Main
1987	J. B. Dunlop
1988	R. G. Cairns
1989	W. J. Main
1990	L. A. Gordon
1991	L. A. Gordon
1992	G. W. Patterson

GULLANE GOLF CLUB CAPTAINS

1882	W. R. Clapperton
1884	T. D. Thomson
1886	J. A. Molleson
1888	H. Parker
1890	J. A. Robertson Durham
1892	D. Turnbull
1894	B. Hall Blyth
1896	John Aitken
1898	Sidney Mitchell
1900	George Dalziel
1902	H. T. N. Hamilton-Ogilvy
1904	A. D. Mackenzie
1906	R. M. Watson
1908	A. W. Robertson Durham
1910	J. B. Stevenson
1912	Lord Dunedin
1914	H. E. Meek
1918	P. J. Pringle
1920	Henry D. Lawrie
1922	J. A. Robertson Durham
1924	Sir Harold Stiles
1926	L. G. Thomas
1928	B. Hall Blyth
1930	T. Drybrough
1932	R. K. Blair
1934	A. O. M. Mackenzie
1936	R. W. Stevenson
1938	Dr J. A. Aitchison
1946	I. H. Bowhill
1948	W. Watson
1950	G. W. Mackie
1952	C. Drummond Stevenson
1954	J. G. Dawson
1956	J. D. H. McIntosh
1958	W. A. Cox
1960	W. F. G. Normand
1962	P. R. Bryce
1964	C. R. D. Leeds
1966	T. D. Hay
1968	G. Robertson Durham

EARLIEST COMPETITION OF THE CLUB

John Deans. W. P. Lindsay. J. Bissett. F. V. Haggart. St. C. Cunningham. W. Elder.
J. D. Thomson. J. P. Croal. Geo. McIntosh, Sr.

T. Lugton, Jr. H. Parker. Drybrough. A. Dawson. Wm. Palmer. H. Bryden. T. Lugton, Sr.
J. A. Molleson. C. Mackinlay. W. W. McCrie. Arch. Murray. Tom Binnie. Robert Chambers.

1970 M. R. A. Matthews
1972 I. A. Ross
1974 R. H. J. Mackie
1976 A. C. Baird
1978 W. C. Morrison
1980 I. A. M. Cowan
1982 E. J. Cuthbertson
1984 D. J. C. Sneddon
1986 J. W. Still
1988 G. W. Paul
1990 A. R. J. D. Miller
1992 H. N. Buchan

POSTSCRIPT

The Centenary of Gullane Golf Club was celebrated with numerous competitions and a dinner at which Lord Derby was the principal speaker.

The Hill will be there for ever. I hope that the greed and folly of man never diminishes its delight.